The Mysticism Of Plotinus

Evelyn Underhill

Kessinger Publishing's Rare Reprints

Thousands of Scarce and Hard-to-Find Books on These and other Subjects!

- Americana
- Ancient Mysteries
- Animals
- Anthropology
- Architecture
- Arts
- Astrology
- Bibliographies
- Biographies & Memoirs
- Body, Mind & Spirit
- Business & Investing
- Children & Young Adult
- Collectibles
- Comparative Religions
- Crafts & Hobbies
- Earth Sciences
- Education
- Ephemera
- Fiction
- Folklore
- Geography
- Health & Diet
- History
- Hobbies & Leisure
- Humor
- Illustrated Books
- Language & Culture
- Law
- Life Sciences

- Literature
- Medicine & Pharmacy
- Metaphysical
- Music
- Mystery & Crime
- Mythology
- Natural History
- Outdoor & Nature
- Philosophy
- Poetry
- Political Science
- Science
- Psychiatry & Psychology
- Reference
- Religion & Spiritualism
- Rhetoric
- Sacred Books
- Science Fiction
- Science & Technology
- Self-Help
- Social Sciences
- Symbolism
- Theatre & Drama
- Theology
- Travel & Explorations
- War & Military
- Women
- Yoga
- *Plus Much More!*

We kindly invite you to view our catalog list at:
http://www.kessinger.net

Because this article has been extracted from a parent book, it may have non-pertinent text at the beginning or end of it.

Any blank pages following the article are necessary for our book production requirements. The article herein is complete.

THE MYSTICISM OF PLOTINUS

IN spite of his enormous importance for the history of Christian philosophy, Plotinus is still one of the least known and least understood among the great thinkers of the ancient world. The extreme difficulty of his style, which Porphyry well described as " dense with thought, and more lavish of ideas than words," together with the natural laziness of man, may perhaps account for this neglect. He was by choice a thinker, contemplative, and teacher, not a writer. Therefore the Enneads, which represent merely notes of lectures hastily and unwillingly written down during the last fifteen years of his life, offer few inducements to hurried readers. The fact that he was a " mystic " has been held a further excuse for failure to understand the more cryptic passages of his works; though as a matter of fact these are the precipitations of a singularly clear and logical intellect, and will yield all their secrets to a sympathetic and industrious attention. His few translators have often been content to leave difficult phrases unelucidated, or surrounded by a haze of suggestive words; and though his splendid and poetic rhapsodies are quoted again and again, even those later mystics who are most indebted to him show few signs of first-hand study and comprehension of his system as a whole. Thanks to this same obscurity, and the richness, intricacy, and suggestive quality of his thought, most of his interpreters have tended to do for him that which he did for his master Plato : they have re-handled him in the interests of their own religion or philosophy. Of this, the Cambridge Platonists are the most notorious example ; but the same inclination is seen in modern

scholars.   Thus Baron von Hügel seeks to introduce a dualism
between his mysticism and his metaphysics.   Even the brilliant
exposition of his philosophy in the Dean of St. Paul's *Gifford
Lectures* is not wholly exempt from this criticism.   A com-
parison of his analysis with those of Baron von Hügel in *Eternal
Life,* and of Mr. Whittaker in *The Neoplatonists* makes plain
the part which temperament has played in each of these
works.

Plotinus himself would probably have been astonished
by this charge of obscurity.   His teaching had by declaration
two aims.   The first was the definitely religious aim of bringing
men to a knowledge of Divine reality ; for he had the missionary
ardour inseparable from the saintly type.   The second was
the faithful interpretation of Platonic philosophy, especially
the doctrines of Plato, and of his own immediate master,
the unknown Alexandrian Ammonius : for his academic
teaching consisted wholly of a commentary on, and interpretation of, Plato's works.   His system, therefore, is a synthesis
of practical spirituality and formal philosophy, and will only
be grasped by those who keep this twofold character in mind.
There must always seem to be a conflict between any closed
and self-consistent metaphysical system and the freedom
and richness of the spiritual life : but since few metaphysicians
are mystics, and few mystics are able to take metaphysics
more seriously than the soldier takes the lectures of the arm-
chair strategist, these two readings of reality are seldom
brought into direct opposition.   In Plotinus we have an
almost unique example of the philosopher who is also a practical
mystic ; and consequently of a mind that cannot be satisfied
with anything less than an intellectual system which finds
room for the most profound experiences of the spiritual life.
In this peculiarity some scholars have found his principal
merit ; others a source of weakness.   The position of his
critics has been excellently stated by Baron von Hügel in
Eternal Life.   He finds in the Enneads a " ceaseless conflict "

between " the formal principles of the philosopher " and " the experiences of a profoundly religious soul." The philosophy issues in an utterly transcendent Godhead without qualities, activity, or being : the mysticism issues in ecstatic union, actual contact, with a God, " the atmosphere and home of souls " whose richness is the sum of all affirmations. Yet, as a matter of fact, this disharmony is only apparent ; and is resolved when we understand the formal character of the Plotinian dialectic as a " way," a stepping-stone, the reduction to terms of reason of some aspects of a reality beyond reason's grasp. The discrepancy is like that which exists between map and landscape. Plotinus, constantly passing over from argument to vision, speaks sometimes the language of geography, sometimes that of adventure : yet both, within their spheres, are true. The Neoplatonic *via negativa* always implies an unexpressed because ineffable affirmation. Therefore its Absolute, of which reason can predicate no qualities, may yet be the " flower of all beauty " as apprehended by the contemplative soul.

Since the doctrine of Ammonius is unknown to us, we have no means of gauging the extent to which Plotinus depends on him : but probably we shall not be far wrong if we attribute to his influence the peculiar sense of reality, the deep spiritual inwardness, colour and life, with which his great pupil invests the dogmas of Platonism. The main elements of the Plotinian philosophy, however, are undoubtedly Platonic. The Divine Triad, the precession of spirit and its return to its origin, the unreal world of sense, the universal soul, the " real " or intelligible world of the Ideas—these and other ingredients of his system are a part of the common stock of Platonism. His originality and his attraction consist in the use which he makes of them, the colour and atmosphere with which they are endowed. That which is truly his own is the living vision which creates from these formulæ a vivid world both actual and poetic, answering with fresh revelations of reality the widening demands and apprehensions of the human soul.

This spiritual world is not merely arrived at by a dialectic process. It is the world of his own intense experience from which he speaks to us; using his texts, as Christian mystics have often used the Bible, to support doctrines inspired by his personal vision of truth. In spite of his passion for exactitude, the sharpness and detail of his universe, he is thrown back, again and again, on the methods of symbol and poetry. We must always be ready to look past his formal words to the felt reality which he is struggling to impart; a reality which is beyond the grasp of reason, and can only be apprehended by the faculty which he calls spiritual intuition. To this we owe the richness and suppleness of his system, the absence of watertight compartments, the intimate relation with life. Whilst many philosophers have spent their powers on proving the necessary existence of an unglimpsed universe which shall satisfy the cravings of the mind, Plotinus spent his in making a map, based on his own adventures in " that country which is no mere vision, but a home;" and his apparently rigid contours and gradients are attempts to tell at least the characteristics of a living land.

Though the Enneads are a storehouse of profound and subtle thought, the main principles on which their philosophy is based are simple, and can be expressed briefly. All things, according to Plotinus, have come forth from the Absolute Godhead or One, and only fulfil their destiny when they return to their origin. The real life of the universe consists in this flux and reflux: the outflow and self-expression of spirit in matter, the "conversion" or return of spirit to the One. With the rest of the Neoplatonists, he conceives of the Universe as an emanation, eternally poured forth from this One, and diminishing in reality and splendour the further it is removed from its source. The general position is somewhat like that given by Dante in the opening of the *Paradiso:*

" La gloria di colui che tutto move
 Per l'universo penetra, e resplende
 In una parte più, e meno altrove,"

though Plotinus would have rejected the spatial implications of the last line, for to him the One was present everywhere. The Divine nature is a trinity; but not, as in Christian theology, of co-equal persons. Its three descending degrees, or hypostases, are the unconditioned One or the Good—a term which implies perfection but carries no ethical implications—the Divine Mind, Spirit, or *Nous*, and the Soul or Life of the World. Nothing is real which does not participate in one or other of these principles. Though the first two hypostases are roughly parallel to the Eternal Father and Logos-Christ of Christian Platonism, and some have found in the Plotinian *Psyche* a likeness to the immanent Holy Spirit, this superficial resemblance must not be pressed. Fatherhood cannot be ascribed to the One save in so far as it is the first cause of life, for it transcends all our notions of personality. Its real parallel in Christian theology is that conception of the " Superessential Godhead, beyond and above the Trinity of Persons," which Eckhart and a few other daring mystics took through Dionysius the Areopagite from the Neoplatonists. The One is, in fact, the Absolute as apprehended by a religious soul. Nor is the Plotinian *Nous* a person, in any sense in which orthodox Christianity has understood that term, though it is called by Plotinus our Father and Companion. Further, the triadic series does not involve a succession either in time, or order of generation; but only in value. The worlds of spirit and of soul are co-eternal with the Absolute, the inevitable and unceasing expressions of its creative activity. The utterly transcendent Perfect manifests as Mind or Spirit (*Nous*); and this *is* the world of being. Mind or Spirit manifests as Life or Soul (*Psyche*); and this *is* the reality of the world of becoming. The lower orders are contained in the higher, which are everywhere present, though each " remains in its own place." " Of all things the governance and existence are in these three."

Whilst every image of the universe is deceptive, since its

true nature is beyond our apprehension, Plotinus invites us to picture the Triad, as Dante did, by concentric circles through which radiate the energy and splendour of the " flower of all beauty," the Transcendent One. " The first act is the act of the Good, at rest within itself, and the first existence is the self-contained existence of the Good. But there is also an act upon it, that of the *Nous ;* which, as it were, lives about it. And the Soul, outside, circles about the *Nous,* and by gazing upon it, seeing into the depths of it, through it sees God " (I. 8. 2). Again, " The One is not a Being, but the Source of being, which is its first offspring. The One is perfect, that is, it has nothing, seeks nothing, needs nothing ; but as we may say it overflows, and this overflowing is creative " (V. 1. 2). Yet this eternal creative action " beyond spirit, sense, and life," involves no self-loss. It is the welling forth of an unquenchable spring, the eternal fountain of life.

As Christian Platonists described the Son as the self-expression of the Father, so Plotinus describes his second Divine Principle as the eternal irradiation of the Absolute—*il ciel che più della sua luce prende.* This principle he calls *Nous ;* a word carrying many shades of meaning, which the older commentators generally rendered as Divine Mind, or Intelligible Principle. Dean Inge has shown good reason for translating it as " Spirit," thus bringing the language of Plotinus into line with the many later mystics who derive from him. As a matter of fact, *Nous* contains both meanings. It is more spiritual than mind, more intellectual than spirit, in the sense in which that word is commonly employed. Those mediæval theologians who made a mystical identification between the Hebrew conception of the Eternal Wisdom as we find it described in Proverbs and Ecclesiasticus, and the Second Person of the Trinity, came very near the Plotinian concept of *Nous,* which is at once Intelligence and the intelligible sphere, Spirit and the spiritual universe; the home of reality, and object of religious and poetic intuition. It is, in one aspect, the " Father and Companion " of the soul (V. 1. 3), in another " the Intellectual Universe, that sphere constituted by a Principle wholly unlike what is known as intelligence in us " (I. 8. 2). This is the " Yonder " to which he so often refers ; the " middle heaven " of Indian philosophy, Ruysbroeck's " clear-shining world between ourselves and God."

"... e questo cielo non ha altro dove
Che la mente divina,"

says Dante; once more condensing the whole Neoplatonic vision in one vivid phrase.

This rich and suggestive conception of the Second Principle, as at once King and Creator of the world of life, and also itself the archetypal world of true values, is the central fact of the Plotinian philosophy. Its apprehension, he says, is beyond ordinary human reason, which is fitted for correspondence with the world of life or soul. It is the function of spiritual intuition; " a faculty which all possess, though few use." Such communion with the world of supernal reality is possible, because man is potentially an inhabitant of it. " The Father-land to us is there, whence we have come : and there is the Father " (I. 6. 8). The " apex " or celestial aspect of our soul is domiciled there. It " never leaves the Divine Mind; but, while it clings yonder, allows the lower soul, as it were, to hang down " (VI. 7. 5). Man is, in fact, intermediary between the two Plotinian worlds of Spirit and Soul, and participates in both. Eucken, in describing him as the meeting-place of two orders of reality, is merely restating the doctrine of the Neoplatonists.

As Spirit is the outbirth and manifestation of the One, so Soul, or Life—the third member of the Triad—is the manifestation or matter of Spirit; and forms the link between the physical and the supersensual worlds. Spirit is " at once its Father and ever-present Companion " (V. 1. 3). Soul is a term covering the whole vital essence (a) of the world, and (*b*) of the individual. It has two aspects. The celestial soul aspires toward, and is in communion with, the spiritual order; the natural soul hangs down and inspires the physical order, thereby conferring on it a measure of reality. We are not, however, to understand by Soul merely the aggregate of individuals. *Psyche* is the divine and eternal life of the created universe, comprehending its infinite variety in a unity which embraces every object in the sense-known scheme, and makes it "like one animal" (IV. 4. 32). It is:

> "A motion and a spirit, that impels
> All thinking things, all objects of all thought,
> And rolls through all things."

The whole creation, says Plotinus, in one of his great poetic passages, is "awake and alive at every point." Each thing has its own peculiar life in the all; though we, because our senses cannot discern the life within wood and stone, deny that life. "Their living is in secret, but they live" (IV. 4. 36). Here we are reminded of the Logos-Christ of the "Sayings"— "Raise the stone and thou shalt find me: cleave the wood, and there am I." By this conception, which is elaborated from the doctrine of the world-soul in the *Timæus*, Neoplatonism bridges the gap between appearance and reality, and also solves the paradox of multitude in unity. "We do not declare the Soul to be one in the sense of entirely excluding multiplicity. This absolute oneness belongs only to the higher nature. We make it both one and manifold; it has part in the nature which is divided among bodies, but it has part also in the indivisible, and so again we find it to be one" (IV. 9. 2).

Soul, which has in its highest manifestations many of the characters of Spirit, is the eternal upholder of the world of change. "Things have a beginning, and perish when the soul that leads the chorus-dance of life departs; but the soul itself is eternal and cannot suffer change . . . what the soul is, and what its power, will be more manifestly, more splendidly evident, if we think how its counsel comprehends and conducts the heavens; how it communicates itself to all this vast bulk and ensouls it through all its extension, so that every fragment lives by the soul entire, which is present everywhere like the Father which begat it" (V. 1. 2). Soul, then, which is in one sense the reality of the world of becoming and immanent therein, is also a denizen of eternity, in virtue of its continuity with and direct dependence on *Nous*. An unbroken series of ascending values unites the world of living effort with the One. It is this which makes the system of Plotinus a philosophy of infinite adventure and infinite hope.

Soul is the lowest of the Divine hypostases. Below it in the scale of values is the material universe to which its lower activities give form, slumbering in the rocks and dreaming in the plants. In plants, says Plotinus, " the more rebellious and self-willed phase of soul is expressed": a doctrine which will find an echo in many a gardener's heart. The sensible beauty of the world is the signature of soul, and points to something "Yonder"; for through loveliness it participates in the world of spiritual values, and we in apprehending beauty turn away from matter to *Nous* (I. 8. 4). Matter, as such, has no reality except as the stuff from which soul weaves up its outward vesture. Deprived of soul, it is in itself, he says, " not-being" and " no-thing": " its very nature is one long want" (I. 8. 5). As a picture is the crude and partial condensation of an artist's dream—all that he can force his recalcitrant material to express—so the physical world is but a fragmentary manifestation of the great and vivid universe of soul, and the body is the smallest part of the real man. When we grasp this, we see how great is the sum of possibilities opened to us by the Cosmos; how easily the country "Yonder" can find room for all the visions and intuitions of artists, poets, and saints.

The Plotinian doctrine of man, which became in due course

the classical doctrine of Christian mysticism, is the logical outcome of this cosmology. Man, like the rest of Creation, has come forth from God and will only find happiness and full life when his true being is re-united, first with the Divine Mind, and ultimately with the One. "When the phantasm has returned to the Original, the journey is achieved" (VI. 9. 11). Hence "our quest is of an End, and not of Ends. That only can be chosen which is ultimate and noblest, that which calls to the tenderest longings of the soul" (I. 4. 6). As the descending stages of reality are three, so the stages of the ascent are three. They are called in the Enneads purification, the work of reason, which marks the transference of interest from sense to soul; enlightenment—the work of spiritual intuition—which lifts life into communion with the eternal world of spirit; and ecstasy, that profound transfiguration of consciousness whereby the "spirit in love" achieves union with the One. These stages are familiar to all students of Christian asceticism, as the codified "mystic way" of purgation, illumination, and union: a formula which Dionysius the Areopagite took from the Neoplatonists. But it is important to remember that in Plotinus this "way" is not—as it sometimes becomes in mediæval writers—a rigid series of mutually exclusive psychological states, separated by water-tight bulkheads. It is rather a diagram by which he seeks to describe one undivided movement of life; a prolonged effort and adventure, which has for its object a deeper and deeper penetration into Reality, the achievement of a true scale of values, in order that the real proportions of existence may be grasped. In this movement nothing is left behind; but everything is carried up into a higher synthesis, as the latent possibilities of humanity are gradually realized, and man grows up into eternal life.

"Since your soul is so exalted a power, so divine, be confident that in virtue of its possession you are close to God. Begin therefore with the help of this principle to make your way to Him. You have not far to go: there is not much between. Lay hold of that which is more divine than this god-like thing; lay hold of that apex of the soul which borders on the Supreme (*Nous*), from which the soul immediately derives " (V. 1. 3).

All practical mysticism is at bottom a process of transcendence, " passing on the upward way all that is other than God " (I. 6. 7) : and this process, in different temperaments, assumes different forms. Since Plotinus united in his own person the characteristics of the metaphysician, the poet and the saint, he tends to present it under three aspects; as the logical outcome of a reasoned philosophy, as a moral purification which strips us of all unreality, and as a progressive initiation into beauty. " Beholding this Being, the Conductor of all existence, the self-intent that ever gives and never takes, resting rapt in the vision and possession of so lofty a loveliness, what beauty can the soul then lack? For this, the beauty supreme, the absolute and the primal, fashions its lovers to beauty and makes them also worthy of love. And for this the sternest and uttermost combat is set before these souls; all our labour is for this, lest we be left without part in this noblest vision, which to attain is to be blessed in the blissful sight, which to fail of is to fail utterly " (I. 6. 7). In the high place which he gives to the category of beauty, which is to him one of the three final attributes of God, the strongly poetic character of his vision of Reality becomes evident. He anticipates Hegel in regarding natural beauty as the sensuous manifestation of spirit and signature of the world-soul " fragment as it were of the Primal Beauty, making beautiful to the fullness of their capacity whatsoever it grasps and moulds " (I. 6. 6) : and those lovers, artists, and musicians who can apprehend it have already made the first step towards the inner vision of the One. Therefore the harsh other-worldliness which made some mediæval ascetics turn from visible loveliness as a snare, would have seemed blasphemy to Plotinus, who would certainly have argued with St. Augustine that " there is no health in those who find fault with any part of Thy creation" (*Conf.* vii. 14). On the contrary, his doctrine gives a religious sanction and a philosophic explanation to those special experiences and apprehensions of artists, poets, and so-called "nature-mystics"—known to many normal persons in moments of exaltation—when

> "The world is so charged with the grandeur of God
> It must shine out, like shining from shook foil."

In such hours, he would say, we perceive through matter the inhabiting *Psyche*, and by it reach out to communion with *Nous*, for "this is how the material becomes beautiful; by participating in the thought which flows from the Divine" (I. 6. 2). He would have understood Blake's claim to see the universe as "a world of imagination and vision," and accepted Erigena's great saying, "every visible and invisible creature is a theophany or appearance of God."

Thus the whole mystic ascent can be conceived as a movement through visible beauty to its invisible source, and thence to "the inaccessible Beauty, dwelling as if in consecrated precincts apart from the common ways" (I. 6. 8). Yet this progress is not so much a change in our consciousness of the world and of ourselves, as a shifting of the centre of our being from sense to soul, from soul to spirit, whereby we come actually to live at new levels of existence. "For all there are two stages of the path, according to whether they are ascending or have already gained the upper sphere. The first stage is conversion from the lower life: the second—taken by those who have already reached the Spiritual sphere, as it were set a footprint there, but must still advance within that realm—lasts till they reach its extreme summit, the term attained when the topmost peak of the Spiritual realm is won" (I. 3. 1).

The process is both intellectual and moral, since its goal is the absolute Truth and Beauty no less than the absolute

Good. "Each must become God-like and beautiful who cares to see God and Beauty" (I. 6. 9). It involves deliberate effort and drastic purification of mind and heart, "cutting away all that is excessive, straightening all that is crooked, bringing light to all that is in shadow, labouring to make all one glow of beauty" (I. 6. 9). As "all knowing comes by likeness" (I. 8. 1), we must ourselves have moral beauty if we would see the "Beauty There." But whether this way be conceived under æsthetic or ascetic symbols, Plotinus is at one with all the mystics in declaring that the driving force which urges the soul along the pathway to reality is love. This inspires its labour, supports its stern purifications, "detaches it from the body and lifts it to the Intelligible World" (III. 6. 5), and gives it at last "the only eye that sees the mighty Beauty" (I. 6. 9). Love means for him active desire; "the longing for conjunction and rest." All shades of spiritual and poetic passion, the graded meanings of admiration, enthusiasm, and worship, are included in it. It is "the true magic of the universe"; an attribute of *Nous*, and an earnest of real life. "The fullest life is the fullest love, and the love comes from the celestial light which streams forth from the Absolute One" (VI. 7. 23). It is true that the impersonal nature of the Neoplatonic One gives no apparent scope to the intimate feeling which plays so large a part in Christian devotion. But the reality and warmth of the true mystical passion for the Absolute—its complete independence of anthropomorphic conceptions—is strikingly demonstrated by those glowing passages in which Plotinus allows his overpowering emotion, "that veritable love, that sharp desire," to speak; and appeals to the experience of those fellow-mystics who have attained the vision of "the splendour yonder, and felt the burning of the flame of love for that which is there to know; the passion of the lover resting on the bosom of his love" (VI. 9. 4). This passion is the instrument of that ecstasy in

which he taught that those men who have " wrought themselves into harmony with the Supreme " may briefly experience the vision of the ineffable One. In it the spirit is burned
to a white heat, which fuses in one single state the highest
activities of feeling, thought, and will. Though the doctrine
of ecstasy appears in Philo, and could reasonably be deduced
from Plato himself, its treatment by Plotinus, the intense
actuality and poetic fervour of its presentation, are the
obvious results of such personal experiences as Porphyry
describes to us. This ecstasy, according to him—and here
he is supported by the majority of later mystics—is not a
merely passive state, nor does it result in a barren satisfaction. When, withdrawing from all lesser interests, the
soul passes beyond all contingency " through virtue to the
Divine Mind, through wisdom to the Supreme," and poises
itself upon God in a simple state of rapt attention, it receives
as a reward of its effort not only the beatific vision of the
Perfect, but also an accession of vitality. At this moment,
says Plotinus, it " has another life " and " knows that the
Supplier of true life is present." The mystic, or " sage," is
not a spiritual freak; but the man who has grown up to
the full stature of humanity and united himself with that
Source of life which is " present everywhere, yet absent
except only to those prepared to receive it " (VI. 9. 4). Therefore he alone can be trusted to be fully active; since his
action is not a mere restless striving after the discordant
objects of a scattered attention, but an ordered movement
based on the contemplation of Reality.

"We always move round the One. If we did not, we
should be dissolved and no longer exist. But we do not
always look at the One. When we do, we attain the end of
our existence, and our rest; and no longer sing out of tune,
but form a divine chorus round the One " (VI. 9. 7).

Yet in spite of the majesty and purity of his vision, the
devil's advocate is not without material for an attack upon

K

Plotinus. The charge brought by St. Augustine against "the books of the Platonists" as a whole—and by these he meant chiefly the Enneads—is well known. He found in their philosophy no response to the needs of the struggling and the imperfect. In its complete escape from the standing religious snare of anthropomorphism, Neoplatonism also escaped from the grasp of humanity. It left man everything to do for himself. For the Christian philosophy of divine incarnation, dramatized in history, and expressed in the phrase "God so loved the world," the Neoplatonist substitutes "So the world loves God." "No one there," says Augustine of their school, "hearkens to Him who calleth, Come unto Me all ye that labour." The One is the transcendent Source and the Magnet of the Universe, the object and satisfaction of spiritual passion; but not the lover, helper, or saviour of the soul. It "needs nothing, desires nothing." The quality of mercy cannot be ascribed to it. As a term, it is as attractive and impersonal as a mountain peak; and the mystic attaining it has something of the aristocratic self-satisfaction of the successful mountaineer. The Christian and Sūfi mystics, even when most deeply influenced by Neoplatonism, have always felt the incompleteness of this conception. They see the soul's achievement of reality as the result of two movements, one human and one divine: a "mutual attraction." "God needs me as much as I need Him," said Meister Eckhart. "Our natural will," said Julian of Norwich, "is to have God, and the good-will of God is to have us."

"I was given," says Angela of Foligno, "a deep insight into the humility of God, towards man and all other things." "The love of God," says Ruysbroeck, "is an outpouring and an indrawing tide." These statements undoubtedly represent a normal element in spiritual experience; that sense of a response, a self-giving on the part of its transcendent object which—whatever explanation we may choose to give of it—is integral to a developed mysticism. Neo-platonism, considered as a religious philosophy, is impoverished by its failure to recognize and find a place for this.

Moreover, the so-called social side of religion, so grossly exaggerated by the amateur theologians of the present day, certainly receives less than justice from Plotinus; for whom the " political virtues " are merely preparatory to the spiritual life, and that spiritual life an exclusive system of self-culture, having as its final stage a " flight of the alone to the Alone." Moral goodness is a form of beauty, and therefore " real "; but there is no suggestion that goodness as such is dearer to the Absolute than beauty or truth. The problem of evil is looked at, but left unsolved: a weakness which Plotinus shares with most mystical philosophers. Evil, he says, has no place in the " untroubled blissful life " of the three Divine Principles. Therefore it is not real, but "a form of non-being " (I. 8. 3): a doctrine which makes an unexpected reappearance eleven hundred years later in the Revelations of Julian of Norwich. Since the aim of the " wise man " is the transcendence of the sense world, there is, moreover, no adequate recognition of those sins, wrongs, and sufferings with which that "half-real" world is charged. Though effort and self-denial have their part in the Plotinian scheme, that transfiguration of pain which was the greatest achievement of the Gospel is beyond the scope of his philosophy. Its remedy for failure and grief is not humble consecration, but lofty withdrawal to that spiritual sphere where the divine element of the soul is at home, untroubled by the conflicts, evils, and chances of life. Even the selfless sorrow of a father or a patriot is to be transcended. Though in this his practice was doubtless better than his doctrine—for we know that he was a good citizen, a beloved teacher, and a loyal friend—he speaks in a tone of icy contempt of those who allow themselves to be disturbed by the world's woe.

" If the man that has attained felicity meets some turn of fortune that he would not have chosen, there is not the slightest lessening of his happiness for that. If there were, his felicity would be veering or falling from day to day; *the death of a child would bring him down*, or the loss of some trivial possession. . . . How can he take any great account of the vacillations of power, or the ruin of his fatherland? Verily, if he thought any such event a great disaster, or any disaster at all, he must be of a strange way of thinking" (I. 4. 7).

Such a sentence, however we look at it, goes far to justify the description of the Neoplatonic saint as " a self-sufficient sage"; and explains the question with which Augustine turned from the Enneads—" When would those books have taught me charity?"

In spite, however, of this fundamental difference in tone, the wider our reading the more clearly we must realize the extent to which the Christian mystics are conscious or unconscious disciples of Plotinus. That unity of witness which is one of the most impressive facts in the history of mysticism, may reasonably be regarded as evidence of the reality of that world of spiritual values which contemplatives persistently describe. But on its literary side, this same unity of witness depends closely upon the fact that these contemplatives, however widely separated by time and formal creed, were able to make plain their adventures to other men by means of conceptions drawn from the Plotinian scheme; which has proved itself able to rationalize and find room for the deepest spiritual intuitions of man. It could do this because a great mystic made it. Hence we find it implied, even where unexpressed, in many of the masterpieces of later mysticism— both Christian and Mahomedan—and some knowledge of it is a necessary clue to the full understanding of these writings. The Sūfi 'Attar, describing the soul's arrival in " the Valley of Unity where it contemplates the naked Godhead," is equally its debtor with the Protestant mystic William Law, declaring that " everything in temporal nature is descended out of that which is eternal, and stands as a palpable visible outbirth of it; so that when we know how to separate the grossness, death, and darkness of time from it, we find what it is in its eternal state." Yet few of the theologians and contemplatives who owe most to Plotinus had any first-hand acquaintance with the Enneads. Their influence reached the mediæval world by two main channels. The first line of descent is through the works of Victorinus and St. Augustine; the second through the philosopher Proclus and his mysterious disciple Dionysius the Areopagite. These lines meet in the *Divina Commedia*, which may be regarded in one aspect as the supreme poetic flower of Neoplatonism.

The dramatic life-history and exuberant self-revelations of St. Augustine have obscured the debt which Christian philosophy owes to that less assertive convert and theologian, Victorinus. Yet since Augustinian Neoplatonism is derived from his writings and translations, he is the real link between Plotinus and the mystics of the Latin Church. A celebrated man of letters and a professor of rhetoric, he had been formed by Neoplatonic philosophy; and is said to have been the author of that Latin translation of the Enneads, which was chief among those " books of the Platonists" that provided St. Augustine's stepping-stones to faith. The stir, not to say scandal, caused by his conversion—so vividly described in the " Confessions"—was justified: for the event was crucial in the history of western Christianity. After his conversion, which took the form of a re-interpretation, not an abandonment, of his old beliefs, he set himself to the creation of a Neoplatonic theology; in which the Plotinian triad, and doctrine of the soul's precession and return to the One, appear almost undisguised. The One he tries to identify with the transcendent and immutable Father. " Son" and " Spirit" are to him two aspects of *Nous*; the fount of all substantial existence, and containing from eternity all things in their archetypal reality. The Son or Logos is "the Logos of all that is," ever gushing forth from the "living fountain" of the Father. It was from Victorinus that Catholicism obtained the characteristic Plotinian notions of Deity as "ever active and ever at rest," and of the life of reality as consisting in immanence, progress, and return, which meet us again and again in the writings of the mystics.

It is plain that St. Augustine, in his first Christian period, was deeply indebted to Plotinus, whom he knew through Victorinus and frequently quotes by name; calling him "one of those more excellent philosophers" whose doctrine of the soul is in harmony with the Prologue of the Fourth Gospel. When he came to write the "Confessions," the glamour of the Platonic vision had begun to fade, and he was able to deal in a critical spirit with his own brief Plotinian experience of "that which Is" (VII. 17). Nevertheless, none can understand that book without some knowledge of the Enneads, from which all its finest passages are derived, and in more than one instance—especially Book VII and the celebrated tenth chapter of Book IX—closely imitated. In Augustine's invocation of "the Beauty so old and so new," in his description of the "Country which is no vision but a Fatherland," or of "the Light which never changes, above the soul, above the intelligence," we see how closely he had studied them, the extent to which their language had permeated his thought. It is, however, in the tracts composed soon after his conversion—e.g. *De Quantitate Animæ*, written about A.D. 388—that their influence is most strongly marked; and the ecstatic vision of the One is definitely put forward as the summit of Christian experience. From this time onwards, the main outlines of mystical theology were more or less fixed: and since St. Augustine was one of the most widely read and deeply reverenced of the Fathers, with an authority hardly inferior to that of Scripture itself, its Neo-platonic colour was never lost. Wherever Christian mysticism passes from the emotional and empirical to the philosophic, this colour is clearly seen, and the concepts of Plotinus, more or less disguised, reappear: even in those mediæval writers who had no direct acquaintance with Greek philosophy. The immense popularity of the so-called Dionysian writings, which derive much of their doctrine through Proclus from the Enneads, helped to establish yet more firmly the Neo-platonic character of Christian and also of Sūfi mysticism. Through these writings the conceptions of the Super-essential Godhead; of successive spiritual spheres or emanations of descending splendour, intervening between the Absolute and the physical world; and of ecstatic union with the transcendent and unconditioned One as the term of religious experience, passed over from the ancient to the mediæval world. Trans-lated from Greek into Syriac in the fifth century, they deeply affected Sūfi philosophy. They entered Western thought in the ninth century, through Erigena's Latin translation. It is said that by A.D. 850 Dionysius was known from the Tigris to the Atlantic: and from this time onwards his influence, and through him that of Plotinus, can be traced in the spiritual literature of Christianity and Islam.

Erigena, whose original works are strongly coloured by Neoplatonism, is the first mediæval writer in whom this influence appears. He follows Plotinus and Dionysius closely in teaching that the Absolute Godhead is " beyond being " and therefore transcendent to the trinity of Persons; a doctrine of doubtful orthodoxy, which was of great im-portance in the later development of mysticism. But a still closer approximation to the thought, and especially to the psychology of Plotinus, is found in Richard of St. Victor: perhaps the greatest mystical theologian, certainly one of the most influential writers, of the early Middle Ages. In

the thirteenth and fourteenth centuries his works, which are
now hardly read, circulated through western Europe, and
shaped the developing mysticism of England, Germany, and
Flanders. Dante, who calls him one " who in contemplation
was more than man," places his radiant soul among those
of the great teachers in the Heaven of the Sun (*Par.* X. 131).
Abandoning alike the many worlds of Dionysius and the
crude dualism of popular religion, Richard taught that three
spheres are open to human contemplation : *sensibilia*, *in-
telligibilia*, and *intellectibilia*—a series closely analogous to
the three worlds of Plotinus. He said that three kinds of
contemplation on man's part corresponded with these worlds.
These are *mentis dilatatio*, a widening of the soul's vision,
which yet remains within the natural order : *mentis suble-
vatio*, an uplifting of the illuminated mind to the apprehension of " things above itself " (or, as Neoplatonists would
say, intelligibles) ; and finally *mentis alienatio* or ecstasy, in
which the soul gazes on Truth in its naked simplicity. Then
" elevated above itself and rapt in ecstasy, it beholds things
in the Divine Light at which all human reason succumbs."
This divine light is the *lumen gloriæ*, the radiance of the
spiritual or intelligible world, which transforms the soul and
makes it capable of beholding God; a conception which
became a commonplace of mediæval theology, was adopted
by nearly all the mystics, and plays an important part in
the *Paradiso*.

> " Lume è lassù, che visibile face
>   lo Creatore a quella creatura
>   che solo in lui vedere ha la sua pace " (xxx. 100).

Ruysbroeck—a student of Dionysius and of Richard—says
of it in *The Twelve Béguines :* " From the Face of the Father
there shines a clear light on those souls whose thought is
bare and stripped of images, uplifted above the senses and
above similitudes, beyond and without reason, in high purity

of spirit. This Light is not God, but it is the mediator between the seeing thought and God." These passages and many like them can be shown to derive directly through St. Augustine from the Enneads. Thus Plotinus says: "Light is visible by Light. The *Nous* sees itself, and this light, shining on the soul, enlightens it and makes it a member of the spiritual world" (V. 3. 8). Augustine, apparently referring to this passage among others, says: "Often and in many places does Plotinus declare, expounding the meaning of Plato, that what they believe to be the Soul of the World has its bliss from the same source as ours, namely, a Light which it is not, but by which it was created, and from whose spiritual illumination it shines spiritually" (*De Civ. Dei.* X. 2). And, of his own ecstatic experience, "I entered and beheld with the mysterious eye of my soul the Light that never changes, above the eye of my soul, above my intelligence. . . . He who knows the truth knows that Light, and he who knows that Light knows Eternity" (*Conf.* VII. 10).

From the thirteenth century onwards, the majority of the mediæval mystics show knowledge and appreciation of those Plotinian ideas which reached them—though in an attenuated form—through St. Augustine, Dionysius, and Richard of St. Victor. Even the Franciscan and Christo-centric enthusiasm of such contemplatives as Jacopone da Todi and Angela of Foligno was affected by these lofty conceptions. Thus Jacopone takes from the Neoplatonists the three stages of spiritual experience, and describes in unequivocal language his successive achievements of that Logos-Christ—so near the Plotinian *Nous*—"*che de omne bellezze se' fattore,*" and of the "Imageless Good" who cannot be named. So too, Angela's successive visions of the divine fullness and beauty, and of "the ineffable Thing of which nought may be said" depend for their expression on the same philosophy.

Nor was its penetrative influence confined to the mystical schools. St. Thomas Aquinas, who accepts and expounds in the *Summa* (I. *q.*12. *a.*5) the doctrine of the *lumen gloriæ*, is considerably indebted to Plotinus in several other particulars; though he cites him inaccurately, and does not seem to have known him at first hand. In a remarkable passage, which afterwards influenced one of the finest rhapsodies of Ruysbroeck, he has actually "lifted" the most celebrated phrase in the Sixth Ennead, and adapted it to the distinctively Christian and non-Platonic view of divine union, as a "mutual act" of God and the soul. "In a wonderful and unspeakable manner," says St. Thomas of the soul in this place, "she both seizes and is seized upon, devours and is herself devoured, embraces and is violently embraced; and by the knot of love she unites herself with God, and *is with Him as the Alone with the Alone.*"

It is in a later and less orthodox son of St. Dominic, the formidable and adventurous thinker Eckhart, that the influence of Plotinus on the mediæval mind is best seen : passing through him to Suso, Tauler, Ruysbroeck, and other mystics of the fourteenth century. Eckhart's philosophy still provides one of the most suggestive glosses upon the Enneads. He made that distinction between the absolute and suprapersonal Godhead and the God of devotion, which was almost inevitable for a Christian thinker trying to find a place in theology for the Neoplatonic One. The Godhead, he says, is "a non-God, a non-Spirit, a non-person, a non-image : a sheer pure One." The Son, in whom "the Father becomes conscious of Himself," combines the attributes of the Logos-Christ with those of the *Nous*. In Him are the archetypes of all created things. There is thus an emanation from the Godhead, through the Son, into creation. The soul's destiny is exactly that conceived by Plotinus : it must ascend to the spiritual world, and through it to its origin, the One, " flowing back into the bottom of the bottomless fountain from which it flowed forth." In Tauler and Suso, and especially in the great Flemish contemplative Ruysbroeck, these ideas—though modified by their inferior speculative ability and more ardent spirit of Christian devotion—are still strongly felt: and since their works and those of their disciples nourished many succeeding generations of contemplatives, through them the mystical side of the Neoplatonic tradition was handed down. In Ruysbroeck, with his threefold division of spiritual experience into "the moral life, the contemplative life, and the super-essential life," and his astonishing and detailed descriptions of the soul's achievement of the Essential Unity, the "death into the One through love," the vision of Plotinus is fully baptized into the Catholic Church. In Jacob Boehme, who drew through Schwenkenfeld and Weigel from Eckhart and his school, the doctrine of the three worlds which forms the basis of his cosmology contains distinct reminiscences of the Plotinian Triad. "These three," he says, "are nought else than the One God in His wonderful works . . . and we are thus to understand a threefold Being, or three worlds in one another." His conception of the Light-world, source of all spiritual beauty and home of "the true human essence," is very near to the *Nous.* Yet the very closeness with which all these mystics follow those parts of the Neoplatonic doctrine which appeal to them, makes it possible for us to measure the distance which separates their minds, their tone and temper, from that of Plotinus and his school. The calm, the austerity of thought, the emphasis on beauty, the clear cool light of the Intelligible World have departed. These men see philosophy through the haze of Christian feeling. Their work is full of passionate effort; is centred on the ideas of sacrifice and of pain. Their religion is coloured by the sharp Christian consciousness of sin, and by the difficulty—never squarely faced—of reconciling devotion to a personal redeemer with the mystical passion for the Absolute. That the philosophy of the Enneads was able to enter a world so remote from its spirit, and come to terms with an attitude of mind in many respects opposed to that of its creator, is an oblique proof of the authenticity of its claim to interpret the spiritual experiences of man.

This is the end of this publication.

Any remaining blank pages are for our book binding
requirements and are blank on purpose.

To search thousands of interesting publications like this one,
please remember to visit our website at:

http://www.kessinger.net

CPSIA information can be obtained
at www.ICGtesting.com
Printed in the USA
BVHW060454011221
622825BV00009B/118